WEALTHY INSPIRATION

THE TANGIBLES AND INTANGIBLES

Vibrancy   Happiness

Radiance   Passion

NWABUEZE OKEKE

Title

Copyright © 2024 by Nwabueze Okeke

Harmony Publishing

Plot 8, Providence Street, Opposite Halifield School, Lekki Phase 1, Lagos, Nigeria.

+2347032212481

publish@harmonypublishing.com.ng

BOOK DESCRIPTION

If you think wealth is just based on the amount of money and properties that one has, then you are wrong on many levels. The truth is that wealth is also based on happiness, brotherliness, the positive impact you have on others, the capacity to learn, language proficiency, achievements, victories, charisma, ideas, innovations and many more.

Wealthy Inspiration: The Tangibles and Intangibles delves into the concept of wealth and aims to make people have a vivid comprehension of the tangible and intangible forms of wealth (the tangibles and intangibles). The book is also intended to make readers realize that wealth is a major source of inspiration, and that wealth is not all about money. Anyone who reads this book would realize that they are the real treasure, and that would motivate them to become a ray of inspiration to others.

INTRODUCTION

Wealth comes in both tangible and intangible forms. Tangible wealth refers to the physical form that can be seen and touched. Examples include money, properties, mineral resources, food and clothing. On the other hand, intangible wealth includes the non-physical, emotional and spiritual form that cannot be perceived by touch or measured in units. Examples include vibrancy, happiness, radiance, passion, love, wisdom, freedom, hope, faith and God's Grace.

Wealth is not only for enjoyment, but also a major source of inspiration. If you use wealth to help and inspire others, then the sky shall be the limit.

TABLE OF CONTENTS

CHAPTER ONE
THE CONCEPT OF WEALTH

Wealth is the large amount of money, properties and assets that a person possesses. It can also be referred to as all those things (material and abstract) that promote the well-being of an individual. There are **two (2)** forms of wealth namely: - **tangible and intangible wealth**. Tangible wealth refers to the physical form of wealth that can be seen and touched. Examples include cash (dollars, pound sterling, euros, francs, rupee, naira); properties (land, farms, houses, cars); mineral resources (gold, diamond, silver, bronze, limestone, petroleum, tin, emerald); food and clothing. On the other hand, intangible wealth refers to the non-material, emotional and spiritual form of wealth which cannot be touched. Examples include vibrancy, happiness, wisdom, freedom, strength, power, good health, emotional intelligence, empathy, comfort, entertainment, confidence, positivity, faith, hope, courage, peace, radiance, love, unity, time, fulfillment, satisfaction and God's Grace.

When a person drinks a bottle of water, the bottle of water is tangible wealth. Whereas the feeling of the person's thirst being quenched is intangible wealth. When a celebrity receives an Oscar award, the award is tangible wealth while the joy, relief and applause that the celebrity experiences while holding the Oscar trophy are intangible wealth. Furthermore, whenever an artist paints, the paintings are tangible wealth because they attract and instill happiness in people who see and touch them. That happiness, together with the artist's imagination and passion, are intangible wealth.

It can be argued that intangible wealth is greater than tangible wealth because unlike money, cars, phones and buildings, it cannot be bought. Money gets depleted until you go broke whereas good ideas win you cool experiences, accomplishments and can even save your life. Furthermore, money is a product of man's creativity; Burglars and con artists strategize first before they execute their crime; The game of chess is all about strategy; Archers and golfers heavily rely on focus and precision to strike their target and win.

For tangibles, beauty is in the eyes of the beholder, but for intangibles, beauty is in the mind and heart of the experiencer. For instance, emerald has a very attractive appearance. But there is much more to the precious stone than meets the eye; its green color symbolizes nature, tranquility, good health, growth, rebirth and hope. However, the green color also symbolizes envy which can jeopardize relationships. Whenever envy tries to sneak in, use the positive intangibles to brush it aside. When a tennis player wins a match or when a footballer scores a last-minute goal, ecstasy and relief quickly spread across the entire stadium. Clocks, wrist watches and hourglasses can get damaged, but time lasts forever; Budgeting is the guiding principle for spending money efficiently; Innovativeness is the mother of new technology; Scientists, architects and engineers cannot perform their work without planning, decision-making and meticulousness; It is wisdom, passion, ambition, determination and perseverance that made **Elon Musk, Jeff Bezos and Bill Gates** the richest people in the world; **Aliko Dangote** is the richest man in Africa but he still aspires and hopes to reach the heights of Elon Musk, Jeff Bezos and Bill Gates. American music star, **Taylor Swift**, won a record **fourth (4th) Album of the Year Award** at the **2024 Grammy Awards**. She was able to achieve that feat due to her talent in singing, hard work, dedication, along with the passion and support from her fans. Because of talent and charisma, **Beyonce Knowles** holds the record for the highest number of Grammy Awards with **thirty-two (32). Lionel Messi** was crowned the greatest footballer of all time (**G.O.A.T**) after his country, Argentina won the **2022 FIFA World Cup**. This was possible due to a combination of intangibles like talent, skill, stealth, teamwork, strategy, hard work, patience, belief, zeal, persistence, luck and courage. Whenever Messi steps on the field, echoes of respect and admiration intensify. **Rafael Nadal** is called the **King of Clay** in tennis because of the unique talent, skill, grit, endurance, tenacity and resilience he displays on the court. It is these intangible qualities that won him an astonishing **fourteen (14) Roland Garros titles**, which is one of the most impressive records in the sport. Whenever Nadal steps on the tennis court, especially on clay, most of his opponents feel intimidated because of his aura of greatness, which Nadal capitalizes on to win matches. The passion from Messi and Nadal oozes and inspires so many players, which forces them to work tirelessly to reach their level: - *Greatness sparks desire, inspires the ambition that drives effort, which leads to more greatness, creating a continuous cycle.*

A person's thoughts are a unique and special intangible. When you are thinking about something, some people want to know what is on your mind and out of curiosity, they ask, *"A penny for your thoughts?"* because they cannot read your mind. That question is a symbolic gesture of interest, care and concern. In fictional movies, superheroes who possessed super intelligence and the ability to read and control peoples' minds (telepaths) are considered the most indispensable and powerful. Moreover, thoughts are what made geniuses like **Albert Einstein, Leonardo da Vinci, Michelangelo, Thomas Edison and Issac Newton** have a tremendous impact on the world. Thoughts are a component of knowledge which is an unlimited intangible wealth. No man is an island of knowledge and due to this fact, every human being must go out, explore and research to know more and discover new ways to expand their horizons. Additionally, the process of learning is a perpetual intangible. It is a continuous process and is one of the most interesting parts of life because as you keep learning, memories are always there to back it up, which is golden. That is why memories can be regarded as an **"invisible treasure box"**.

There are other words which represent wealth (synonyms). They are: - **affluence, riches, treasure, fortune, luxury, enormity, opulence, welfare, abundance, plentitude and multitude.**

CHAPTER TWO

THE CONCEPT OF TANGIBILITY AND INTANGIBILITY

TANGIBILITY

Tangibility refers to the attribute of being perceptible to the sense of touch or possessing physical form or substance. In the context of finance, billing, accounting, corporate finance, business finance book-keeping and invoicing, tangibility plays a crucial role in determining the nature and characteristics of various financial assets and liabilities. It serves as a fundamental concept in evaluating and classifying items that have a physical existence, enabling businesses and individuals to assess their financial positions accurately.

The concept of tangibility lies at the heart of financial measurement, facilitating the distinction between tangible and intangible assets. Tangible assets are those that have a physical form and can be touched, felt, or seen. These assets include real estate properties, machinery, equipment, inventory, and vehicles. On the other hand, intangible assets lack physical substance and represent rights or privileges. Examples of intangible assets include patents, copyrights, trademarks and goodwill.

Tangibility also extends to liabilities. Tangible liabilities are obligations that require the physical payment of assets or the performance of specific actions. Examples of tangible liabilities are accounts payable, loans, leases and salaries payable. In contrast, intangible liabilities do not involve physical payments but rather obligations that are difficult to quantify or measure precisely, such as warranties, legal claims and contingent liabilities.

The concept of tangibility is closely related to financial reporting and valuation. When preparing financial statements, businesses must consider the classification and recognition of their tangible assets and liabilities, adhering to accounting standards such as **Generally Accepted Accounting Principles (GAAP)** or **International Financial Reporting Standards (IFRS).** The valuation and measurement of tangible assets include historical cost, fair value and revaluation model, depending on the specific asset or the accounting framework employed.

Tangibility also impacts various financial ratios and analyses, allowing stakeholders to assess a company's financial health and stability. For instance, the tangibility ratio compares a company's total tangible assets to its total liabilities and shareholders' equity, providing insights into the proportion of tangible assets supporting the firm's obligations. This ratio aids investors, lenders and analysts in evaluating the level of asset coverage available to satisfy potential claims.

In the realm of business and corporate finance, tangibility influences decision-making processes. For instance, when a business seeks financing, lenders or investors often consider the presence of tangible assets that can serve as collateral or security. Tangible assets provide a sense of security and reduce risk for those providing funding, as they offer potential recourse in case of default or insolvency.

In conclusion, tangibility is a key concept in finance, billing, accounting, corporate finance, business finance book-keeping and invoicing. It plays a crucial role in distinguishing between tangible and intangible assets and liabilities, impacting financial reporting, valuation and analysis. By considering the tangible aspects of financial items, businesses and individuals gain a better understanding of their financial positions and can make informed decisions to promote stability and growth.

INTANGIBILITY

Intangibility refers to the lack of palpable or tactile property making it difficult to assess service quality. According to **Zeithaml et al.** (1985), *"Because services are performances rather than objects, they cannot be seen, felt, tasted or touched in the same manner in which goods can be sensed".* As a result, intangibility has historically been seen as the most important distinction between services and products in the literature on service marketing. In practice, service production and consumption often involve both intangible and tangible elements. Examples of intangible service attributes include service responsiveness and reliability, while tangible service attributes include the services cape, décor and furnishings.

A drawing on **Construal Level Theory (Ding and Keh, 2017)** investigated when and why intangible versus tangible attributes would be more influential in service evaluation. They showed that under a high construal level, consumers rely more on intangible attributes in their service evaluation and choice formation, whereas under a low construal level, consumers rely more on tangible attributes in their service evaluation and choice. Furthermore, the effect of construal level on service evaluation can be explained by imagery vividness, and these effects are moderated by the type of service (e.g. experience vs. credence services).

When a customer is buying a service, they perceive a risk related to the purchase. To reassure the buyer and build their confidence, marketing strategists need to give tangible proofs of service quality. In addition, there is evidence that certain service industries already apply intangibility versus tangibility strategies as a function of construal level. For example, firms selling retirement insurance policies often target young workers who are a few decades away from retirement. Their advertising seeks to convey to the viewer ideas about retirement based on their insurance services and tends to use taglines that highlight company longevity and company reputation. Moreover, service firms consider their physical distance from their customers. For example, a community shopping center emphasizes its tangible attributes such as accessibility of location and variety of stores. In contrast, a catalog or mail order retailer that does not have a physical outlet and emphasizes on intangible attributes such as responsive service and assurance of product delivery to attract customers.

CHAPTER THREE
QUOTATIONS ON WEALTH

"It is the heart that makes a man rich. He is rich according to what he is, not according to what he has". - **Henry Ward Beecher**

"Not he who has much is rich, but he who gives much". - **Erich Fromm**

"We are rich only through what we give, and poor only through what we refuse". - **Anne Sophie Swetchine**

"Wealth belongs to the person who enjoys it and not to the one who keeps it".

"Powerful! There's so much strength in you and me". – **Jussie Smollett**

"Memories are there to back up the things we have learnt".

"Ideas are the currency of the new economy". – **Richard Florida**

"It is not what we take up, but what we give up, that makes us rich". - **Henry Ward Beecher**

"To stay alive, it's mind over matter. To feel more alive, it's heart over matter".
"Make no mistake, my friend, it takes more than money to make men rich". - **A. P. Gouthey**

"The real measure of our wealth is how much we'd be worth if we lost all our money". – **John Henry Jowett**

"Religion is a means of empowerment and unity. The friendship between Christians and Muslims is gold".

"God gave us wealth, not that we should be hoarders but dispensers". – **Thomas Manton**

"No man is an island of knowledge; hence the desire to go out, explore and discover new ways to expand your horizons".

"It's simple arithmetic; your income can grow only to the extent that you do". – **Harv Eker**

"Good communication is as sweet as sugar and as stimulating as black coffee". – **Anne Morrow Lindbergh**

"Money is only a tool. It will take you wherever you wish, but it will not replace you as the driver". – **Ayn Rand**

"Once solidarity is firmly established and felt, it becomes unbreakable and paves the way for feeling more alive, thus making it the perfect solid".

"True wealth is not of the pocket, but of the mind and of the heart". – **Kevin Gates**

"Your hospitality hit me hard and I learnt a thing or two".

"Passion is energy. Feel the power that comes from focusing on what excites you". – **Oprah Winfrey**

"I've got money on my mind, but I have to work for it". –
Liam Payne

"Time is more valuable than money. You can get more money, but you cannot get more time". – **Jim Rohn**

"I found that wealth requires either willpower or why power, and the latter is often the real source of the former". – **John Soforic**

"It's the passion flowing through the veins; it's the moment you remember you're alive; it's the air you breathe, the element, the fire". – **Nelly Furtado**

"Here's to the ones that keep the passion, respect. Here's to the ones that can imagine, respect, oh yeah, hayya o!". – **Jungkook**

"Euphoria, take my hands now, you are the cause of my euphoria. Oh yeah! When I'm with you, I'm in utopia". - **BTS**

"Without the rich heart, wealth is an ugly beggar". - **Ralph Waldo Emerson**

"Chop my money. I don't care because I get plenty wealth".
– P. Square

"Wealth can do us no good unless it helps us toward heaven". – **Thomas Adams**

"The two great tests of character are wealth and poverty".

"There is nothing like seeing the smile on my kids' faces. Playing and laughing together. It's the best". – **Mark Wahlberg**

"I look one side and unity is felt; I look the other and it's shining victory".

"Once you find that peace, harmony and confidence, that's when you start playing your best". – **Roger Federer**

"I stopped thinking too much about what could happen and relied on my physical and mental strength to play the right shots at the right time". – **Novak Djokovic**

"Some sports give a lot of emotions because you know the people well, not personally but they express their passion

and their emotion on the field so you have an attraction". –
Patrick Mouratoglou

"The more you praise and celebrate your life, the more there is in life to celebrate". – **Oprah Winfrey**

"No matter what happens in life, be good to people. Being good to people is a wonderful legacy to leave behind". –
Taylor Swift

"Madea is a Southern term. It's short for mother dear. The truth is there are a lot of Madeas out there". – **Tyler Perry**

"Darling boy! I'm so proud of you". – **Vivi Wonder**

"If you have a good mother, then you have won the lottery". – **Jeff Bezos**

CHAPTER FOUR

THE WHITE AFFLUENCE THEORY

"*Every good-hearted human is motivated to earn wealth through noble means, with* white affluence *instantly becoming a target as the highest level of wealth attainable. It outshines dark affluence (obtained through fraudulent means) in all aspects by being the radiating bedrock of happiness, freedom, comfort, power, dominance, stability, fulfillment, fame, fortune, good health, respect, inspiration and blessings from God and Allah*".

Nwabueze Okeke

ILLUSTRATION OF WHITE AFFLUENCE THEORY

AFFLUENCE

Earned through industriousness, wisdom, strategy, grace, love, optimism, hope, passion, focus, patience, perseverance, tolerance, integrity, humility, honesty, gratitude, resilience, empathy, commitment, philanthropy, discipline, self-control, confidence, faith, financial management, time management, divine favor.

EFFECT

happiness, freedom, comfort, power, dominance, stability, fulfilment, fame, fortune, good health, inspiration,

DARK AFFLUENCE

Acquired through theft, armed robbery, lies, bribery, blackmail, embezzlement, extortion, drug and human trafficking, ransom from kidnappings, forgery, cybercrime.

CONSEQUENCE

corruption, greed,
hatred, conflict,
instability, remorse,
imprisonment.
shame, life
sentence.

CHAPTER FIVE
HOW WEALTH CAN INSPIRE

Inviting God into your life.

Inviting Allah into your life.

Accomplishing and winning.

Using your talents and skills to help people.

Being kind.

Being empathetic.

Being lucky several times.

Surprising people in a cool way.

Delivering motivational speeches.

Enthusiasm in learning and teaching others.

Through good mentoring.

A lifestyle with positive impact.

Listening to inspirational music.

Watching motivational films.

Flipping through photo albums.

Taking a trip down memory lane.

Valuing history.

Governments allowing democracy to reign.

Receiving good news or valuable information.

Admiring drawings, paintings and other art works.

Appreciating and feeling connected to nature.

Jubilating with others wholeheartedly.

Writing and researching with all your heart.

Being cheerful and positive.

Engaging in teamwork.

Defying the odds.

CHAPTER SIX
THE ROAD TO WEALTHY LIVING

Smooth planning.

Making the right decisions.

Being optimistic.

Putting on a smiley face.

Maintaining good health.

Improving yourself in new ways.

Living in the moment; not thinking too much about the past and the future.

Embracing brotherliness.

Taking the easy way out sometimes to reduce stress.

Realizing that some things are as easy as ABC.

Seizing the opportunities that fortune presents.

Being brave.

Entertaining yourself and others.

Making people laugh occasionally.

Achieving goals with sheer determination.

Channeling your inner strengths.

Keeping the hope alive.

Unwavering faith.

Being happy and content with who you are.

Accepting that life is not perfect.

Learning from mistakes.

Igniting the passion.

Being inspired.

Being empowered.

Seeing a bright light at the end of the tunnel.

CHAPTER SEVEN

WHAT WEALTH MEANS IN DIFFERENT

LANGUAGES

The meaning of "Wealth" in various languages

French – Richesse

Portuguese – Fortuna

Spanish – Poder

Italian – Ricchezza

Latin - Divitiae

Arabic – Tharwa ثروة

Chinese – Caifu 财富

German – Reichtum

Irish – Saibhreas

Dutch – Rijkdom

Norwegian – Rikdom

Swedish - Rikedom

Greek – Ploutos

Romanian – Bogatie

Serbian – Bogatstvo

Swahili – Utajiri

Yoruba – Oro

Hausa – Dukiya

Igbo – Aku na uba

Vietnamese – Su giau co

Polish – Bogactwo

Slovak – Bohatstvo

Croatian - Bogatstvo

Czech - Bohatstvi

Welsh – Cyfoeth

Filipino – Kayamanan

Georgian – Simdidre

If you memorize all these translations, you will feel inspired because a different language symbolizes a special kind of communication and a new perspective of life. After pronouncing these translations with vigour, you will feel cooler than mint. Language proficiency reflects the character growth of its speakers. Additionally, the knowledge and fluency of languages is a famous breeze that passes through the learning environment and pushes you to success.

REMARKS

Wealth is not just for pleasure, but also a beacon of inspiration. Use the tangibles efficiently, focus more on the intangibles and allow yourself to be inspired. This is the key to the Hall of Wealthy Inspiration which can open many doors to feeling more alive. Anytime you touch money, raise trophies and use fancy gadgets, always remember that it is vibrancy, excitement, jubilation, compassion, generosity, gratitude, motivation, fulfillment and inspiration that penetrate the heart. Moreover, this book is a product of ideas and was written with sheer ambition.

AUTHOR BIOGRAPHY

Nwabueze Okeke is a Nigerian born in Jos, Plateau State in 1991. He is a Christian who hails from Anambra State and belongs to the Igbo tribe. Furthermore, Nwabueze is the last born in his family. In 2014, Nwabueze obtained a bachelor's degree (BSc.) in Economics from Caritas University, Enugu State. He also obtained a master's degree (MSc.) in Human Resource Management in 2016 from Sheffield Hallam University, the United Kingdom (UK).

Nwabueze is very passionate and intellectually motivated. He has great enthusiasm for foreign languages including Portuguese, French and Spanish. It is with sheer passion that Nwabueze decided to write the book, *"Wealthy Inspiration: The Tangibles and Intangibles"* with the hope of inspiring people worldwide.

www.ingramcontent.com/pod-product-compliance
Lightning Source LLC
Chambersburg PA
CBHW070137230526
45472CB00004B/1579